Custom Cars
IN COLOR

Richard Nicholls

octopus

CONTENTS

*The 'Damn Yankee' lays down a fine burnout at the
top end of the strip in the best traditions of drag racing
(endpapers); a V12-powered Ford Model T
(title page) is here pictured at rest; the blown
350 cu in Corvette Stingray was built for the rock star
John Bonham (left).
Cover picture: A Ford Model T-bucket with a
Chrysler Hemi-powered engine.*

INTRODUCTION

'Custom Car' is not a term you will find in a dictionary. Even to those familiar with the world of custom cars there has always been a problem in defining exactly what is, or is not, a true custom car. For simplicity, therefore, every effort has been made to keep the material and the explanations clear and straightforward. With this in mind the whole range of custom cars has been divided into four groups which are by no means exact or clear-cut. To begin with, any vehicle in any of the groups would qualify for the description of 'custom car', but they are all much more than just that. The style and appearance of any of them is broadly based on part of the history of motor racing, and from the evolution of the sport has come the evolution of the custom car.

The roots of customising lie in the 1920s and 1930s and have a stronger association with California than anywhere else, particularly with the successive younger generations of the past 30 years.

Beginning with the early racers who first competed in stripped-down Model T Fords on dirt ovals, and moving from there to the 'hot-rodders', which raced on the dried-up lake beds and between junctions on their home streets, the sport graduated to established and purpose-built tracks in America and all over the world, and drag racing became the top-class entertainment and spectacle it is today. Along the way the development of the cars left a legacy of alterations to body and engine which are often seen on custom cars for purely cosmetic reasons. All of these owe their existence to the search for more and more speed along the straight quarter-mile, whether it be the common aerodynamic spoiler which is factory-fitted to so many production saloon cars, or the pronounced rear-end 'hike', still only used by the racer or the die-hard customiser.

In the early days of racing, particularly the immediate post-war period when money was short but the old cars of the thirties were cheap and plentiful, the youngsters all had 'wheels'. Racing on the street was widespread, but illegal, and soon moved to off-road 'strips'. While they were still trying to get recognition as a serious form of motor sport, the early drag racers had to use their cars

'Small Fry' (right) *is a 1937 Austin Ruby with a blown (supercharged) Rover V8 engine.*

4

every day on the road as well as for weekend racing. The cars had to be capable of fulfilling both functions as they stood or at least to be swiftly and easily changed from runabout to racer and back again. Some of the cars, set up for racing but driven on the street, looked so dramatic that their appearance was copied simply for the visual effect, and it was at that moment that customising began.

This was originally a treatment applied to the cars of the 1930s, and for some that period still retains its magic, giving birth as it did to that classic vehicle the Deuce (1932 Ford). The favourite and most common cars from that period are mainly those which came from the Ford production line in such great numbers that many examples, from the Model T onwards, still survive in good order today.

Apart from being, roughly speaking, custom cars, these older models have another, more accurate description. To the enthusiast, any car which was manufactured before 1949 and has a flat or split windscreen is a 'rod'. Originally a 'hot-rod', which applied to the souped-up racers, and now also a 'street-rod', 'rod' has become the preferred form of description.

After 1950 the situation becomes less clearly defined, and although we have called all the post-1950 cars 'street machines' for ease of reference, it is not completely correct, and owners of some of the classic fifties cars might well feel a little upset. Strictly speaking, a street machine can be any post-1950 car, as modern as this year's model, which has been altered from standard in appearance and has performance which far outstrips that originally intended for it. This can most easily be achieved by a straightforward engine swap, substituting a bigger, more powerful unit, but the pleasure which many enthusiasts derive from 'tweaking' or tuning a factory engine to increase its power output is very much in evidence here.

The influence of drag racing on these cars is obviously very strong, and raises an interesting point. Although the roots of customising are closely bound up with the development of drag racing, and although there is a class of drag racing specifically for street cars, it is probably impossible to find a purpose-built racer which is either legal, or even practical, for street use. By the same token, few owners of beautiful custom vehicles would risk their destruction by racing them.

A Chevrolet small-block engine (right) *is fitted here into a Bucket T. 'The Saint'* (below) *shows its racing muscle.*

RODS

Probably the most graceful and elegant period of car design was the years between the Model T going into production and 1951. The classic cars of this time provide the raw material for the modern-day rodder. Whether it be the hardy annuals like the Ford Model T, the Model A and B, or something rarer like this 1933 Ford Tudor (*below*), the flowing lines and natural beauty of these cars allows ample scope for anyone to produce a real star of the road.

Probably the most commonplace (if that is the right word for any of these cars) rod on the roads of Britain is the once-humble Ford E93 Popular (*below*). Known affectionately and simply as the 'Pop', the description of 'sit-up-and-beg' distinguishes it from later models of the same name. The fact that so many of them were made accounts for the large number of survivors still available to rodders, and although the number must be limited, it seems that more and more of them pop up every week. In fact there are so many appearing at car shows that there is often a separate category set aside for them in the judging, quite an honour on the car-show circuit.

No-one at Ford, or even the early owners, could possibly have imagined the way the cars look today. Stiffening of what was once a very flexible chassis allows the fitting of larger and more powerful engines – the Rover and Daimler V8s are favourites – as well as the use of sophisticated modern suspension and steering components, leaving the car a practical road-going proposition.

In most cases it is only the body which remains as in the original, and new parts, either steel or glassfibre, can be easily obtained. But since the use of wider wheels demands the fitting of wider wheel arches, and the narrow pillars make the chopping of the roof a fairly simple operation, very few of them have even the body shell in common with the factory specification.

Then of course there is the paintwork. Here the flat, almost square bootlid of the Pop presents a ready canvas for the mural artist to exercise his skill (*below right*). Most often, in what is still a confined space after all, the application of a cartoon sketch or motif seems to work best. And since it is common enough for owners to give their cars a name, these little designs are often used to reflect the name of the car to good effect. From this sophisticated use of the airbrush and other painting techniques has sprung the theme car, in which the whole concept of the vehicle is decided on before the work begins and bodywork, colour scheme and mural are in the one style.

The open-bodied Bucket T has always been a favourite, and 'Andromeda' (*top left*) is a prime example of a total project in which no effort or expense has been spared in the search for perfection, from the handbuilt suspension to the huge blown V8 engine. Not a single piece of metal on the car has escaped the eagle eye of the builder or the chroming vats, and the paintwork is flawless. As ever, it is attention to detail which marks a show winner.

The street 'digger' T (*left*) owes everything to drag racing and is a classic example of the neccessities of the strip being transferred to the street for purely cosmetic reasons.

Despite its immense length, somewhere in excess of 5m (17ft), the car was built for everyday use on the street and that is exactly what it gets. The owner has constructed a fine blend of eyecatching shock and practicality. It even turns corners!

A typical example of one of the most famous rods ever, the Deuce Coupe (*above*), was immortalized by the Californian singing group The Beach Boys. The name 'Deuce' comes from the year of manufacture – 1932 – and it represents one of the all-time classics of rodding, the Ford Model B. Almost as common in America as the Pop is in Britain, steel Model Bs are few and far between outside the United States; only a small number were ever exported. Like the one in the picture, most of the export models are glassfibre, which does not take anything away from its appearance.

The Ford Model Y (*above*) was made during the 1930s by Ford of England, based on the American Tudor (page 8) and remarkably similar to it in appearance. Like the Tudor, these cars are comparatively rare these days, and the value of genuine steel originals reflects their scarcity.

Thanks to the growing interest in rodding on a worldwide basis, and also to more sophisticated techniques in the production of glassfibre panels, replicas of this and other rare cars are now more easily available. The construction of new, stronger chassis has long been a standard in rodding, and is even offered on a factory production-line basis. Although the more dedicated builder will probably prefer to do it all himself from the ground up, the combination of the two means that no car, however old or rare, need be lost to future generations.

There are still some cars around which seem to be unique, though, and Lady Luck (*top right*) is a beautiful example. It is a 1935 Hillman, and the body, although it has been extensively restored after rust had nearly eaten it away, is still original in appearance – no roof chops for this classic.

The other option open to the rodder is the use of new sheet steel to replace body parts which have been damaged or have decayed. This can usually only be successful on body panels which are flat – double curves like those on wheel arches are much harder to reproduce without the benefit of a press and the original moulds – but it does retain the authentic flavour of the car rather more than glassfibre panels. Attempts to partly restore old rods are definitely increasing. The idea is to produce a car which looks as much like the original as possible, but, by the addition of a more powerful engine and modern running gear, has all the reliability and comfort of the modern saloon car.

The 1932 Model B Sedan (*right*) is a fine example of this. Only close examination reveals that the car sits lower on the road than stock, and still closer examination shows that it has been channelled and the body sits lower in the chassis than before. Also, no factory original from Ford was ever fitted with a small-block Chevy engine, but still the 'genuine' feel persists. The Bucket T, 'Boston Strangler' (*overleaf*) looks more unusual.

The similarity between the Ford Model A (*top right*) and the later Model B (*bottom right*) is fairly obvious. The easiest way to spot the difference is to look at the radiator shell – a chrome item on the A and an enclosed part of the body on the B. Even those, however, are interchangeable.

There is no mistake about the Model T. By far the most common form the T takes is the open, or Bucket version (*below*). The familiar brass radiator shell with its Motometer on top marks out all temperature variations, and the upright steering column is another sure trademark.

Henry Ford could not have anticipated what he was starting when he first put the T into mass production all those years ago, and the modern counterparts, unlike the early production models, are anything but black in colour. If you look at the picture you can, thanks to the open-plan engine and suspension layout on the car, see all the traditional signs of a classic rod. The tube front axle, suspended on a transverse leaf spring, is a mass-produced item these days, and can be ordered to suit the car with ends to take a wide variety of wheel fittings from almost any manufacturer. The brass headlamps are unlikely to be original, but replicas are available (as they are for the radiator shell) and there are so many glassfibre bodies available too that the choice can be bewildering. The Model T comes in many other forms as well – such as the pick-up, centre-door, open 'bucket', C-cab delivery van – and they all are much loved by the customiser.

STREET MACHINES

The fifties saw the beginning of a new era in car design;
it was from then on that production techniques enabled
the use of double-curved wrap-around windscreens and
the totally enclosed wheels which are still with us. The
days of grace were arguably over, but the modern cars,
like this 1969 Chevrolet Impala, had potential of their own.

At first glance there seems much less scope for customisers with the post-1950 cars, and it would appear that this type of car is forever doomed to the addition of a few bolt-on goodies like chin spoilers and lamp bars. However, this would be underestimating the apparently limitless imagination of the enthusiasts. The custom builder has two basic choices to make here: he can either keep the car as close to stock as suits his purpose, or he can throw convention out of the window and go for an all-out street racer.

The Mk I Cortina (*above*) represents a sort of halfway house between the two, proving again that you cannot confine the cars completely within a fixed set of rules. Although the builder has kept all the major bodylines of the factory original, there are some more subtle changes, like the rear lights, which certainly are non-standard items, as is the central filler cap. The wide rear tyres and the beefed-up rear end (raised by the use of longer spring shackles) both have their roots in drag racing and give the clue to the nature of the engine and the purpose of the builder.

The much-altered Morris Minor (*right*) also runs a bigger-than-stock engine, although the builder has managed to squeeze it under the bonnet without leaving any visible traces. Such bodywork alterations as have been made are very restrained and tasteful.

Among the more modern custom cars it is already obvious that plenty of room for variety exists, and out of that variety come one or two fairly distinct styles. Perhaps the most dramatic in appearance is the Lowrider – a type which is so far almost exclusively confined to certain parts of America. The term is descriptive enough, and the aim is to turn your car into a 'pan-dragger' and get it as close to the ground as is mechanically possible as with this Lincoln Lowrider (*above*). Recently it seems that the best way to achieve this is by the extensive and expensive use of hydraulics, most of which are borrowed from aircraft, and which act on the suspension of the car in the same way as the hydraulic ram of a tipper truck. This method offers infinite and minute control of the ride height of the car from the driver's seat, allowing the car to be raised at one, two, three or all corners at will. The latest fad in lowriding is hopping – making the front of the car jump off the ground by use of hydraulics alone, and it says much for the power and sophistication of the units that jumps of about one metre are quite common.

With cars capable of being lowered right onto the ground – although usually only when parked –

very often they have castors fitted underneath to prevent damage to engine and running gear.

The Vauxhall Victor (*top right*) has also had some suspension modifications made, but these are strictly related to performance. The small but noticeable hike to the rear end improves weight transfer as the car pulls away and gives more traction to the rear wheels. This is very important to the serious racer.

A faint hint of the same effect is visible on the 1957 Chevrolet (*bottom right*), but it is not so pronounced, and little has been done to alter the lines of the classic car. The V8 Chevrolets from 1955, 1956 and 1957 are as important and indispensable to the street racer and customiser as the Model B and T Fords are to the rodders.

All the production saloons from the Chevrolet stable shared the same designer over those years, and 1955 was the year that Chevrolet introduced their revolutionary small-block V8 engine, which ever since has been the bread and butter of the engine builder on both street and strip, providing high power output and good tuning potential in a compact, lightweight package. This made the '57 model in standard trim good value for money.

Probably the most commonly used V8 engine is
the small-block 350 Chevy, which is standard
equipment in Camaros and Corvettes. Properly
treated it can give phenomenal power, and better
still responds well to the addition of a blower. Not
only does this add speed to the car, but a nicely
chromed blower has considerable visual appeal,
rising, as it almost always has to, through the
bonnet of the car, often raising the carburettor
into the driver's line of vision (*overleaf*). The blower
also makes a powerful whistle, clearly audible
above the thump of the exhausts; seeing it and
hearing it are every bit as rewarding as the power
bonus it brings to an engine. One glance at the
glittering Camaro engine (*above*) should be enough
to convince any sceptic.

Of course, there is much rivalry between the
supporters of different camps. There is no shortage
of admirers for the Ford Mustang and its variations
on the V8 theme. Steve McQueen made the
Mustang famous in its early form, but it is the
Mach I wedge-shape (*right*) which seems to be
most popular. The early cars are much prized as
well, particularly in convertible form or with the
massively powerful Shelby Cobra engine, which is
physically too large to be fitted into later models
without major changes under the bonnet. For-
tunately, the 351 Cleveland engine variation
provides as much power and potential as anyone
could wish, and it fits as well.

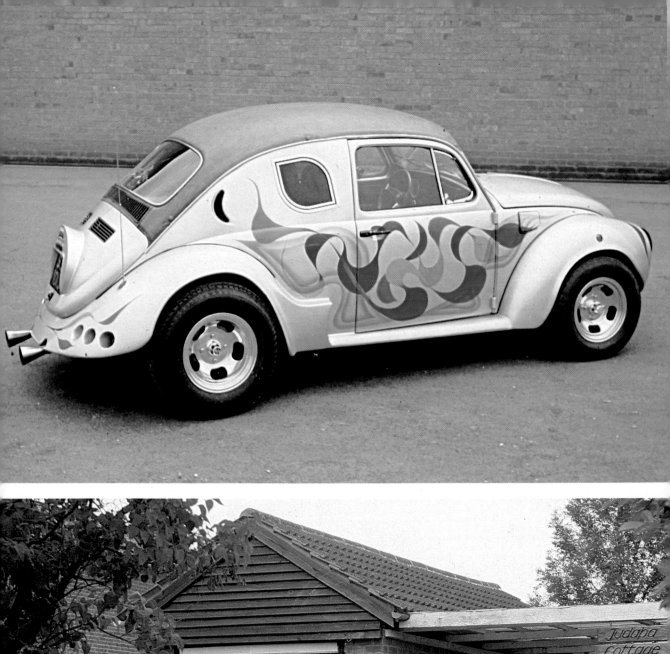

Power is not the only interest of the customiser though, and many cars, which at first sight may appear to be relatively humble, offer huge opportunities to anyone with the will to be different. The Beetle (*above left*) is a surprising target for this sort of treatment. It may be simply due to the vast numbers of these cars that have been made (19 million and still rising) which make them so frequent a contender, or it may be that some people find its squat, humpy appearance genuinely attractive. Among the modern cars it is as much of a diehard as the Pop and the T are to rodders.

The floorpan and engine, as a self-contained unit, have been a favourite base for anyone to build a mass-produced kitcar on, and the seemingly immortal Beach Buggy is the best example of this. But the original Beetle is still good value and responds well to a restrained and sympathetic approach. Blanking of the rear windows, lowering, de-seaming and repainting make a dramatic change in appearance, and wide wheels, with correspondingly flared wheel arches, and perhaps even a small roof chop, emphasize its dumpy shape even more. And, of course, the vastly more powerful Porsche engine is virtually a bolt-on

extra, turning the ordinary 'people-car' into a screamer that could easily outrace anything in the neighbourhood.

There are many cars with a sort of hidden class which may not be initially obvious. The early English Ford Mk I Zephyr and Zodiac (*above*) are prime candidates in this category, and once again sympathetic treatment, in which the existing shapes are emphasized and accentuated, is the best answer. Other points in their favour include the fairly wide availability of replacement parts and the fact that the once derided slab-sided appearance makes the repair of rusted panels by the use of sheet steel well within the capabilities of the majority of enthusiasts. Couple that with a strong chassis and the interchangeability of nearly all Ford engines and you have a winner.

Some cars, though, have what can only be described as natural class. Take the 1951 Mercury (*bottom left*) as an example. The huge, gleaming, 'juke-box' front end has a style all its own; put a coin in the slot and maybe it will start playing early fifties rock'n'roll! There is not much you can do to a car like that except keep it clean and polished and enjoy it.

CUSTOM CRAFTS

Every sport or hobby has its own secrets. To the outsider the jargon of something as simple as football or cricket can seem like another language, while to those directly involved it is simplicity itself. The custom world has its own terminology, of course, and the confusion begins right away because almost anything could be called a custom car, and yet have another description which is better and more accurate.

We have already covered this ground with *rods* in the introduction without ever mentioning the *resto-rod*, a subdivision of the class tending more towards subtle restoration rather than eyecatching modification, and we have touched briefly on the confusion among the later cars, which may or may not be *street machines*. *Vans* are self-explanatory, although it would be a mistake to forget the humble pickup – once a tradesman's workhorse, now a cult vehicle in its own right – and it is simple enough to place the many categories of *competition vehicle* in one group. About the only common factor among the various groups and sub-divisions is the fact that they all share a similar terminology.

Most of this terminology is based on the American drag-racing influence and is therefore less puzzling to an American than it is to a European. For example, the Englishman will call what are effectively (and originally) the mudguards of a car 'wings'. To an American, and thus to a custom enthusiast, they are *fenders*. It follows then that the detachable shrouds over wheels (usually at the back, but just as possibly the front ones too) are known as *fender skirts*. In similar fashion, the bonnet becomes the *hood*, and the boot the *trunk*.

Now the subject becomes more complex. Many of the cars and vans have been treated to what is probably the single most dramatic and popular body modification, the *roof chop*. This involves lowering the roofline of the vehicle by cutting several centimetres out of the roof supports and door pillars and replacing the entire roof section on the shortened remnants. A good deal harder than it sounds, chopping looks tremendously effective and also offers some streamlining advantages.

Sectioning is the same thing at a lower level. Involving the removal of a chosen amount of the actual bodywork below the window line, effectively it means that the car is cut in half horizontally, the chosen amount of body is removed and the top half replaced on the bottom half, leaving a lower, sleeker profile. Performed with sympathy, it can be hard to detect and most appealing in appearance. Because of the difficulty of the task it is relatively rare.

Channelling takes place at a lower level still, and calls for the body of the car to be mounted lower on the chassis than is usual. This lessens ground clearance and reduces the overall height of the car. It may also require that the car floor be removed and repositioned inside the body. It is a fairly rare car which has been chopped, channelled and sectioned, although many have one or two of these modifications. The improvement in appearance repays the effort involved many times over once the job is done.

Another way that ride height (that is the height of the car floor from the ground) and overall height can be reduced is by repositioning the axles and suspension. The *tube axle*, which is exactly that, is traditional for the front suspension, and by bending the ends upwards during manufacture a *drop tube axle* is produced. Fitted to the car, it will mean the chassis, and thus the bodywork, sit closer to the ground. Similar adjustments at the back are somewhat harder, mainly because the back axle has to supply power to the rear wheels. Since most cars which undergo a rebuilding process like this also get fitted with a more powerful engine in the process, the standard back axle is very often scrapped as unsuitable. To purists, the best replacement is an independent rear suspension

IRS) like that which is standard on the big Jaguars. Supported as it is in a simple 'cage' of steel, the IRS can be fitted to most chassis with relative ease, and its mounting position can be chosen to give the ride height desired, high or low. As a bonus the IRS, with its inboard disc brakes, short driveshafts and spinning universal joints, responds well to cleaning, painting or chroming and improves the rear aspect of any custom car.

It is by no means the only rear axle in use, and the solid axle can also be smartened up easily. And, by the use of lowering blocks, or by repositioning the suspension mountings themselves, or by the more complicated *Z-ing* of the chassis, which involves cutting and rewelding the chassis rails, the height of the car can be altered to suit the builder. The use of hydraulic pumps and rams can allow the driver to alter the ride height at will, even while driving.

The amount of variation in ride height and angle has settled into a few well-accepted styles over the years, and the terminology is self-explanatory as it reflects their appearance closely. Thus we have the *Highrider* and the *Lowrider*. These terms are usually taken to apply to newer cars, while similar-looking rods are more likely to be called *Highboy* (or *Hi-boy*) and *Lowboy* respectively, although they would need more than just suspension changes to qualify fully for those titles.

From the more obvious changes in appearance it is a short step to the multitude of minor alterations which are in common use. *Nose and decking* is one which tends to suit the big cars of the fifties better than the rods for very good reason. It involves the removal of the superfluous body decorations, badges and trims of which they had so many. The subtle effect can be very pleasing, but it depends on a straight, clean and well-painted body for its success.

The thoughtful use of louvres – small slots with raised and curved edge – can improve the look of almost any car, old or new, but they must be pressed out of a steel panel on a special machine. Because of this, and despite their versatility, they are limited to the smaller, flatter parts of the car bodywork which can be detached and placed in the machine. They are most often seen on fender skirts and the flat-sided hoods of the pre-fifties rods.

Frenching is perhaps the most common body modification of all, as it is simple enough to perform and adaptable enough to suit any car or van. Most often it is side and tail lights which are treated in this way, but it suits radio aerials, number-plates and headlamps just as well. Any external feature which normally stands away from the bodywork can be frenched simply by setting it into a recess, to any depth required. The bigger the object, the harder the operation becomes, which is why side lights and aerials are the most common subjects.

Simple though it is, frenching is not the easiest modification to make. That honour falls to a simple change of wheels, which is usually the first thing on the list for a customiser and the last thing for a rodder. There are many types of wheel available, and they are often called different things by different manufacturers, although in general the terminology is easy enough to follow. In the main wheels are made from a lightweight alloy – magnesium has a good strength-to-weight ratio – and are cast with slots, spokes or similar good-looking patterns. Thus we get *slot mags*, *dish mags*, *wire mags* and so on – a bewildering range of options.

Bewildering also is the full list of words and phrases which are involved in custom building. It would take an encyclopedia to cover the subject fully, which is another way of saying that we have so far only scratched the surface, and then not very deeply. Sufficient terms have been included to provide a basis of understanding which will enable you to enjoy the cars both in photographs and on the road.

VANS AND PICK-UPS

Big vans and small vans ought really to be nothing more than utility delivery vehicles. But the van is a cult vehicle in its own right. Luxuriously trimmed inside in leather, velvet, or anything else, fitted with cocktail bar, refrigerator, plush seating and even bedding, it offers complete freedom and mobility to the owner, as well as a large mobile platform for the mural artist to decorate. This big Chevy demonstrates the idea rather well.

The pickup, though hardly a car, is not really a van either, and perhaps, in view of its popularity, deserves a place of its own. It is a strange combination of parts, offering no more comfort to the driver than a small sports car, being a strict two-seater, and having as much storage space for luggage or the weekend shopping as a handbag. A tonneau cover over the pickup bed will provide weather protection of sorts, but hardly makes it the safest of places to keep the family jewels. In truth the pickup is probably the most impractical vehicle for everyday use.

The heavy lines of the British Austin A55 (*above*) have been sensibly used to create a custom vehicle in the classic style, and it is not so much the things that have been done to the vehicle as the things that have not that make it as pleasing to the eye as it is. Aside from a roof chop, the body remains as the factory built it, but that, combined with the lowering of the suspension all round, has definitely changed the character of the whole vehicle. A simple, one-colour paint job puts the finishing touch and makes it individual and very classy.

The Model B pickup (*top right*) is a glassfibre replica on a modern chassis and relies on its original style for its success, providing an entirely different solution to the same problem.

The small van, like the little Escort (*bottom right*), has to work entirely differently, as the builder has to relieve the slab sides to get away from the utility vehicle image. The small, porthole-style windows on the side are a quick answer, and are available as factory-made items in a wide variety of shapes and sizes which, though mass-produced, offer the individual a chance to be different. The use of two windows either side, reflecting the window area of the rear door, combined with the lettering of the van's name along the side, do the trick very neatly.

The Fordson van, 'Speed Freak' (*overleaf*) has arrived at a similar solution through the application of graphic striping kicked up over the rear wheels and echoing the flared wheel arches. These are clearly much wider than any factory-produced part, but again, the van can fall back on its flowing shape to catch the eye.

The Morris 1000 pickup, 'Night Driver' (*above*), is yet another example of restraint. The road to success is paved with people who know when to stop. It reflects also a growing modern trend towards semi-restoration and preservation of the vehicle for its own sake. An engine change, to give more power than the tiny original, is by no means apparent, and about the only visible differences are the wider wheels and the slightly flared arches to accommodate both the wheels and English motoring law. The effect that makes this car special is the lovingly applied pearl paint and the monochrome toning murals along the sides and back of the pickup bed. The effect of the pearl paint, like so many of the other paint finishes, is extremely hard to capture photographically, and is seen to best effect under sunlight, when it glistens and shimmers, changing colour as it passes by.

That is not to say that the pickup will not respond to drastic alteration, like the little Chevy 'Luv Machine' (*top right*). Dramatic, contrasting striping over a bold colour follows the body line of the vehicle, which sits lower and wider than stock. The wrap-around chin spoiler and the removal of bumpers and chrome trim adds to the effect and is in keeping with the overall feel of the vehicle.

The pickup (*bottom right*), with its narrow bed and external wheel arches, adds a new dimension of toughness to an otherwise flat surface.

The big van offers a whole new world to the imaginative mind, perhaps mainly because of its sheer bulk externally, and the almost limitless opportunities which the interior area allows. This Bedford CF (*left* and *above*) has been given almost every kind of treatment available. The small-block Chevrolet engine gives it the kind of road-going performance and flexibility which might be expected of a reasonably powerful saloon car, but can pull it when loaded at a relaxed pace. The Jaguar axle can cope with all the power the engine can give, but chromed and painted, manages it all with eyecatching style and appeal.

The standard wheel arches, flared to good effect, hold the wide wheels well and give extra strength to the squared-off shape of the van, while the paint is the icing on a most attractive cake. Inside, what was once a vast storage area has been transformed into a comfortable combination of passenger seating and relaxed luxury. A small amount of cupboard space, attractively fitted and panelled, includes a cocktail cabinet, while the blue velvet finish to all the seating and the dash makes the general specification sound like something from an estate agent's housing list rather than a motor vehicle. With all that space, individual preference makes possible any combination of television, bar, refrigerator, gun rack, cocktail cabinet, seating and bedding.

With all that flat metal outside, it is hardly surprising that the big vans are often the most dramatically painted vehicles on the road. The paint serves two purposes here; pure decoration, usually on a chosen theme in keeping with a name, and as a means of relieving what could be a dull, heavy shape. The CF van 'Odessa' (*below*) is a show-winning example of the former. It incorporates all the advantages of a big van, including an engine swap for a more powerful V8, but has also been used as a mobile canvas for an expression of something more than that. The sea battle at Odessa was historically important, and the builder has used it as a theme on which the muralist has enlarged. It works here on a big van when it could not possibly succeed on anything smaller. Not everyone likes murals of course, and their execution calls not only for artistic ability, but considerable specialist skill in application and use of the airbrush – a sort of tiny paint spray-gun – which may be outside the ability of the average builder.

A big van can be relieved in other ways though, either by the simple use of windows (*top right*), which cuts down on the amount of plain steel, or by the use of striping to accentuate existing body shapes, which is also illustrated on the van at the top right.

As an alternative to striping it is equally possible to contrast parts of the body by the use of large different-coloured areas (*bottom right*). This tends to deceive the eye in much the same way as camouflage paint on military vehicles, although with a completely different aim in mind and much more attractively. Rather than emphasizing body shape, it alters it slightly, creating a kind of optical illusion. The paintwork is always finished off with several coats of clear lacquer.

The van itself is not a limiting factor which has to be worked round and allowed for, rather it can be treated radically for the pure fun of being different and ever so slightly silly. 'Little Tuff Nut' (*above*) is a clear indication of this. Essentially a Honda TN7, this midget pickup has been transformed into a satisfying strip performer (though a highly impractical street vehicle) by the simple, if drastic method of putting a blown 3-litre V6 engine in the back, where only empty space previously existed. The tiny size of the vehicle meant that the engineering problems were immense – the Jaguar rear end is belt driven and installed backwards, but it goes.

'High Roller' (*top right*) has been altered at a basic level, and is indicative of the growing interest in off-road vehicles. Apart from the big V8 engine which has replaced the factory in-line four, even an unpractised eye can tell that it has been lifted up on its suspension to give the greater ground clearance which rough terrain demands if serious damage is to be avoided.

The sumpguard adds to this protection, as do the steel brush bars running up around the front. Bolted directly to the chassis the bars are strong enough to withstand all but major impact, and provide a firm mounting base for a small but powerful winch. This could haul the van or one like it out of deep mud should it ever become bogged down or stuck.

Airbrushed artwork decorates the Dodge van (*right*).

LEE ELIMINATORS

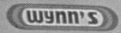

CRAGAR

COMPETITION CARS

As 'Stardust' burns out at the top end of the strip, warming its tyres prior to a full pass down the magic quarter-mile, we come back full circle to drag racing. This is the most spectacular of all forms of motor sport. It is extremely demanding in terms of concentration and offers the most punishing treatment an engine can take. This is where the art of customising began.

The early hot-rodders, racing between road junctions or traffic lights, started the whole thing off, and drag racing has grown from there, never looking back. From the humblest of street classes (page 61) at a local strip, to the Top Fuel Funny Cars racing at international level, the purpose of drag racing is the same; the fastest possible standing-start race over a very short quarter-mile (400m) strip of tarmac. Like the gladiators of ancient Rome, it is a one-to-one contest in which there is no runner-up, only a winner and a loser, and the winner takes all.

The flipped-up Funny (*top left*) shows all there is to see; a Funny Car is only a chassis and an engine with a glassfibre body perched on the top – a dragster with a little extra. But it is most often the Funnies that draw the crowds and their staggering performance is the obvious reason why.

'Blue Max' burning out (*bottom left*) gives a clear impression of just how spectacular these cars can be, but unless you have stood next to the track and felt the ground shaking and your ear-drums bursting as a pair of Funnies leave the line, a photograph can only be a pale imitation of the real thing.

In September 1979, Gene Snow and Ray Beadle, at Santa Pod in England, laid down the fastest ever side-by-side Funny Car run in history. The winner went through in six seconds dead, travelling at more than 350km/h (220mph). Although liquid traction compounds, applied to the track and tyres, make burnouts an unnecessary luxury (*above*), the drivers still enjoy doing it as much as the crowds enjoy seeing it. The effect is certainly spectacular and that is what the fans want; seven million fans in the USA alone.

It is not only the Top Fuel cars which bring in the crowds, of course. Many people go to watch the sort of car they can personally relate to, even though the noise and drama may not be as shattering. There is a definite thrill in watching cars like 'Al's Gasser', an apparently ordinary Pop, shaking and twitching with suppressed power on the line before the lights on the 'christmas tree' run through their sequence to green and the front wheels lift clear of the ground as the car snakes down the strip in a blast of pure power (left).

Looking at the Pop, all the tricks of the road-going cars are there: the high back end, with its much larger tyres, puts power down on the ground where it is supposed to be, and the 'wheelie bars', poking out at the back, stop the car from flipping over onto its roof at the launch.

When cars are evenly matched, as they should be, and the only real difference is the ability and reaction time of the driver, the launch from the start line (above) is where the race is won or lost. For that reason the starting lights on the tree flash through their sequence at a variable speed which can be dialled in from the race director's box, so that the lapse between amber and green can be different every time. Likewise, the race director can dial in a handicap, as each driver has his own set of lights, to allow for cars of different weights and capability to run together without unfair advantage. Thus, from the time the light goes green until the moment the car passes through the timing traps at the far end of the strip and pulls his 'chute (overleaf) to slow the car, it is driver against driver.

It is not only the driver who can win or lose the race; preparation of the car and engine is just as important. The chassis of any car is its first critical factor, and it is capable of the same sort of fine tuning as the engine itself, in the same way that modern Formula One cars can be adjusted to suit any particular track or set of road conditions. Rivalry for expertise and finesse is as high among chassis-builders as it is among drivers. The mechanics – those people who know which end of a spanner is which – are also vitally important and

there are annual awards now in Britain for 'Mechanic of the Year'.

Dennis Priddle (*below*) has gained renown as both a driver and a chassis-builder, and this picture shows one of his early mid-engined rails which has now been superseded by the rear-engined configuration as the lessons of experience have been applied to the cars themselves.

Almost as vital again are the pit crew. They are the overalled men who run out beside the car as the driver burns out in preparation for his run,

guiding him backwards (or pushing in the case of classes which do not need a reverse gear to qualify) into a central spot on the strip (*top right*) and checking his helmet, belts and 'chute before his pass (*overleaf*).

Getting any one of those things wrong can mean the difference between winning and losing, or even more; as in all forms of high-speed competitive motorsport, life is at stake, and it says much for drag racing that loss of life is so low in this area of motor sport.

The Street classes of drag racing are those which are most closely allied to the grass roots of the sport, in the days when the kids used the same car on the strip at weekends as they did on the street during the week. In theory all the street cars should be capable of use on the public highway, although the theory does not always match up to the practice. With the engine tuned for short bursts of power from the moment of takeoff, the cars are totally impractical for everyday use, being almost uncontrollable in traffic or rain, although exceptions do exist. In general, though, the Street class is nothing of the sort; imagine driving any of the cars on this or the previous page down to the local shops. The closest thing to the original drag racing car is the Roadster class, which is aimed directly at the private individual with a car he believes is capable of sufficient effort to make an impression. Although this class of racing is slower than the rest, it does enable the original relationship to continue.

The customising trend is growing all the time in all areas of the sport. The European scene is dominated by Britain and Scandinavia, although customising is not as widespread there as it is in the United States of America. The sport of drag racing in the USA is centred on Indianapolis and, to a lesser extent, California.